1
Remember, Remember!

Guy Fawkes stared up at the waiting hangman. He shivered, but not with fear. The January wind blew icy cold.

He caught the eye of his close friend, Thomas Winter. "Be brave, Tom!" he cried over the noise of the crowd.

"Farewell!" came the reply. "Till we meet again in a better place."

Guy shook his head. He could
think of so many better places to be.
He remembered running as a boy in
the green dales of Yorkshire… and
in the city of York where he was born
in 1570, thirty-five summers ago.

He remembered getting into mischief at school with Jack and Kit Wright. They were both dead now. They were killed after the failure of the Gunpowder Plot – surely the greatest piece of mischief ever planned.

Memories returned, too, of the years spent in the dales village of Scotton and the visit once to nearby Knaresborough with Tom Winter.

They had dared each other to go inside Mother Shipton's cave. Everyone said she was a witch.

Later, outside the cave, they had shared the same secret wish at the magic well. "I wish to become a soldier," Guy had repeated after Tom, "and help to make England a Catholic country once again."

Now Guy watched sadly as Tom was pushed towards the scaffold by the guards. The crowd roared loudly and began the popular, mocking chant to taunt the men who were about to die:

"Remember, remember,
The Fifth of November,
Gunpowder, Treason and Plot.
We see no reason,
Why Gunpowder Treason,
Should ever be forgot!"

Guy could hardly believe it was really happening to him. "How did I get myself into this mess?" he wondered bitterly. "How did it all start...?"

2
Keep it Secret

It had begun back in 1604, when Guy had received a surprise visitor at his army camp. It was his old friend Tom Winter. They were both soldiers in Europe, but they rarely had the chance to meet.

"I'm homesick, Tom, and tired of war," Guy confessed. "I wish sometimes that I had never become a soldier."

At first it had all seemed like a great adventure to Guy when he joined the Catholic Spanish army to seek his fame and fortune. But things had not worked out for him as well as he had expected and now he wanted to leave.

"Why not come back to England with me?" Tom suggested.

"Who has need of me?" Guy asked with interest.

"The Catholics of England. King James has begun to pass cruel laws against our Faith. We must help our people."

"But what can I do?" asked Guy.

Tom checked that no one else was listening. "Remember the second part of our boyhood wish?" he asked in a hushed voice. "Together we can help to make it all come true..."

So Guy went back with Tom. They
met some more old friends at a
London inn. There was Jack Wright
and Thomas Percy, once a neighbour
at Scotton. The ringleader was a
man called Robert Catesby.

Everyone gave an oath of secrecy, by resting a hand on the Bible. Then Catesby explained his plans. "We are going to blow up the House of Lords with gunpowder!" he began. He looked each man, in turn, in the eye to win their trust. "As King James makes his speech to Parliament, he and all his Protestant supporters will be killed." Catesby's eyes glowed brightly.

"What will happen after that?" asked Guy, wide-eyed.

"An armed force will then be ready to ride upon London. The victory will be ours and soon there will again be a Catholic monarch on the English throne," Catesby replied.

Guy gulped. He knew there was no turning back now. He must do what must be done – or die in the attempt.

Percy rented a house next door to Parliament and the plotters tried to dig a tunnel between the two buildings to smuggle in all the gunpowder. It was a difficult task for so few men to carry out, especially when the narrow tunnel kept filling with water.

"Aargh, my aching back!" Tom groaned. "This heaving and digging will be the death of me."

Tom and Guy looked down at their blistered hands. "We have been scraping at stone for weeks," Tom sighed. "I fear the wall is too thick and we will never be able to get through."

But in early 1605 they found
that they did not need to finish
the tunnel after all. A storeroom
had become empty in the cellars
below the House of Lords – right
underneath the King's throne!

3
Bomb Warning!

"Steady! Be careful!" hissed
Catesby in the darkness.

Kit Wright grinned.
"Do not worry. We will not let
the gunpowder get wet!"

Kit helped his elder brother, Jack, lift another heavy barrel of gunpowder from the boat towards the cellars.

"Good, now put it over there with the others," said Guy, holding up his lantern to guide them. He was in charge of the explosives.

Boatload after boatload of
gunpowder was rowed across the
river that night until thirty-six
barrels were stacked in the cellar.
Guy made sure that they were
completely hidden by mounds of
coal and firewood.

"You have done well, my friend,"
Catesby praised Guy warmly.

"You deserve to light the fuse to set
off the huge explosion, Guy. Then
your name will go down in history!"

Guy laughed. "People will only
remember me if I am stupid enough
to blow myself up, as well!"

During the months of preparations that followed, Catesby persuaded a number of wealthy Catholics to enter the Plot too. They promised to provide money, horses, armour and weapons after the King was dead.

But there was a fear that if too many people knew about the Plot, there would be a greater risk that the King might find out.

Nevertheless, the explosion was planned for the opening of Parliament on Tuesday, the fifth of November.

But one fateful Saturday in late
October, a letter was sent, unsigned,
to Lord Monteagle, a Catholic friend
of several of the plotters. The letter
warned Monteagle not to go to the
opening ceremony.

Monteagle took the message
straight to the Government's
chief ministers.

It read, "…they shall receive a terrible blow, this Parliament, and yet they will not see who hurts them…"

When Catesby heard about the warning, he refused to scrap his plans.

No one knew for certain who had broken their oath and written the note. But the main suspicion fell upon Francis Tresham.

He was the thirteenth and final member of the gang. He was also Lord Monteagle's brother-in-law.

Tresham denied it, and Catesby ordered Guy to guard the cellar alone.

At midnight on the fourth of November, Government troops searched the cellars. They found Guy there – with the explosives, the fuse and the match. He had been caught red-handed.

4
I am not Afraid to Die

At first Guy said nothing to his
captors. He didn't give his name or
any information about the other
plotters. Now that the Plot had
failed, Guy wanted to allow his
friends enough time to escape.

Guy was taken by boat to the Tower of London and slung into a tiny, dark cell called Little Ease. He could not even stand up or lie down.

Over the next few days, information was slowly forced out of him by torture. Guy's body was stretched and broken on the rack, the most feared instrument of torture in the Tower.

Finally he could stand the terrible
pain no longer and confessed all that
he knew about the Plot. Guy was
almost too weak by now even to
be able to sign his own name.

His courage had been wasted.
Unknown to Guy, his friends had
all been captured or killed during
a shoot-out at Holbeach House
in Staffordshire.

Guy wept when he heard the news. Four of them had been shot dead – Catesby, their leader, Percy and both the Wright brothers. Tresham died in his cell from poison.

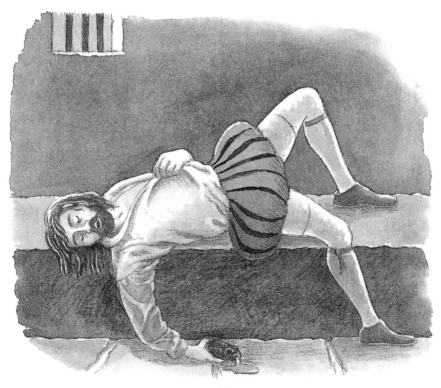

The rest were brought to the
Tower and quickly found guilty
of High Treason for plotting to
kill the King.

On the actual night of the
fifth of November, the people of
London celebrated the failure
of the Gunpowder Plot.

They lit bonfires and threw straw figures of Guy Fawkes into the flames to see him burn.

Now, on the last day of January, 1606, the crowd was screaming for his blood.

It was too late for any more hopes and dreams. This was the end.

Four men were to be hung, drawn
and quartered that day.

Tom was the first to mount the
hangman's scaffold. "I die a true
Catholic," he cried out.

A large crowd had gathered.
Everyone wanted to see the traitors
executed, especially Guy Fawkes.

They did not have to wait for
long. Guy was the last man to kneel
in front of them all.

He made the sign of the cross
and prayed out loud, "I ask the King
and God for forgiveness."

His life was over. But the fame of
Guy Fawkes would live on for ever.